Now and Here

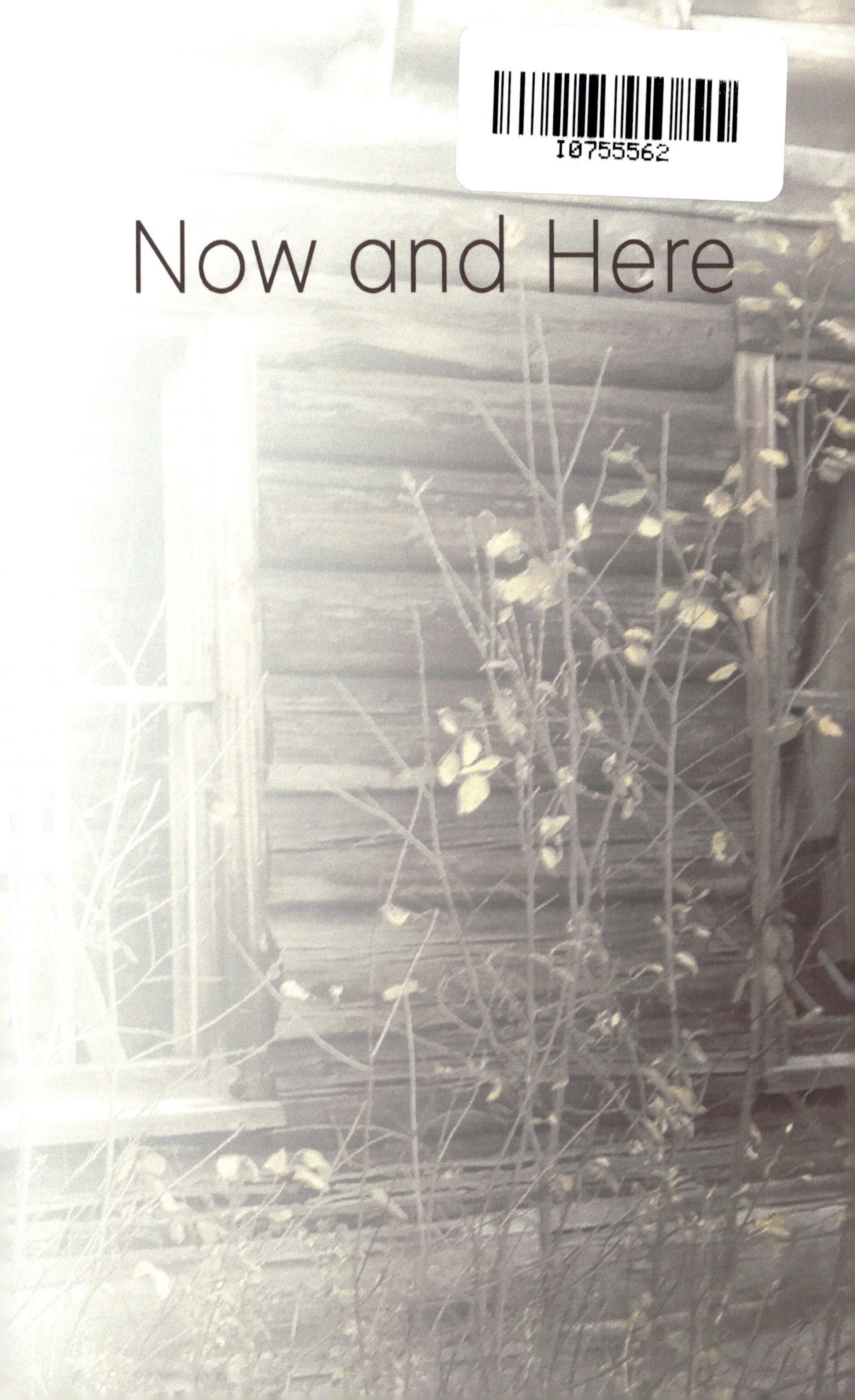

Now and Here

poetry by

Naomi Beth Wakan

photography by

Christine Brooks Cote

SHANTI ARTS PUBLISHING
BRUNSWICK, MAINE

Now and Here

Published by Shanti Arts Publishing
Interior and cover design by Shanti Arts Designs

Shanti Arts LLC
193 Hillside Road
Brunswick, Maine 04011

shantiarts.com

Printed in the United States of America

ISBN: 978-1-956056-09-9 (softcover)

Library of Congress Control Number: 2021947871

"Men esteem truth remote, in the outskirts of the system, behind the farthest star, before Adam and after the last man. In eternity there is indeed something true and sublime. But all these times and places and occasions are now and here. God himself culminates in the present moment, and will never be more divine in the lapse of all the ages. And we are enabled to apprehend at all what is sublime and noble only by the perpetual instilling and drenching of the reality that surrounds us."

—Henry David Thoreau, *Walden*

Reflections on Tanka

by Naomi Beth Wakan

Most people have heard the word *haiku* and may even be familiar with this Japanese three-line poetry form. *Tanka*, which I use here to accompany Christine's photography, are five lines, but they should not be considered "stretched haiku."

Tanka, though they are the parents of haiku, are very different creatures. During tanka parties, poets would sit around and take turns first offering three lines of poetry and then alternating with two lines—the five lines of a tanka. The most important poet in the group would start this poetry game, often preparing those first three lines prior to the gathering rather than offering them spontaneously; the poet wanted to ensure an impressive start. Those first three lines would often describe the moment of the event, using images from nature. Eventually those three lines split away and became haiku. This happened about 400 years ago.

Tanka developed about 1000 years before that and are, in fact, the longest continually written form of verse known. Around 800 C.E., the Japanese started developing their own written language instead of using the imported Chinese one. *Uta* (songs) became less Chinese and more Japanese in style, and tanka (or *waka* as they were called at that time) grew out of the *uta*. Some *waka* developed independently, but sometimes a long song would finish with a coda, a kind of summing up of the whole thing, and from these coda also came the *waka* (tanka).

Haiku is always written in the present tense, so writers of haiku catch a moment in time and become one with what they are describing. With tanka, the poet pulls back from the object they are describing, and in its five lines, the tanka can tell of the past, imagine the future, give moral judgments, and offer philosophical comments on the ways of humanity.

Although tanka were used mainly for communication between friends and lovers in Heian times (794–1185), for me they are the perfect form for expressing life's ephemeralness, dissatisfaction with longings never fulfilled, and nostalgia for a time that probably never occurred.

> longing always
> for a home, that even
> when I now have one,
> I still feel myself with
> a residual longing

Tanka aren't really complete sentences. Denis M. Garrison describes them as "the middle of the story." The first word isn't capitalized, leaving open where the tanka is coming from, and there is no period after the last word. This leaves the reader's thoughts free to wander where they may.

For me, tanka is a form that allows my inner life to open to my outside life. An outer image strikes me—in this case, Christine's photos present an image for me to consider—and almost immediately it triggers some inner emotion or idea, so I record that beneath the image description. The tanka facilitates this by often having a pivot line. The pivot line, usually the third line, hangs in the air, as it were, turning me from my objective description to my subjective reaction. The pivot line has to make sense with the first two lines it follows—the upper section, *kami-no-ku*—as well as the last two lines—*shimo-no-ku*—it precurses. It enriches each section as well as revealing their connection. The pivot line turns the tanka from the external "Aha!" moment of haiku, to an internal "so that's the way it is!"

Whether a tanka pivots from its upper to lower section with a segue pivot line or whether it just tumbles down from line to line like a glorious waterfall, the tanka excels in one thing, and that is integrity. No posturing in tanka as the poet tells of the world as they see it.

Because the poet's presence can be more than implied in the tanka, Sanford Goldstein comments on them as "behind the scenes, the autobiographical moments of the poet." Whatever inspire tanka—love, longing, loneliness, nostalgia—it is its humaneness that makes it such a wonderful form of poetic expression. Tanka present a self-awareness and a coming to terms with life's ups and downs. Often the best ones blend nature with humanity, and so Christine's wonderfully moody nature photographs are the perfect stimuli for my writing.

Reflections on Photography

by Christine Brooks Cote

Photography crept up on me. For most of my life, I wasn't the least bit interested. I wasn't much interested in the visual arts in general . . . to look at them, yes, but not to do them. My parents made sure I had an education in the musical arts—piano, flute, and voice lessons—but I grew up thinking I had no talent for the visual arts.

I acquired my first digital camera around 2005. It wasn't large and fancy, just a little point and shoot. But the fact that it was digital was a big deal. I didn't have to take the film to a drugstore to pay to have it developed. I could develop the pictures myself, so to speak, on the computer. And I could take a lot of photos and toss out the ones I didn't like. I could experiment and see which I liked best. I could crop pictures and remove things I didn't want in the picture, like power lines and signs. I could soften colors and add some blur or haziness to a photo if that appealed to me. These technological advances changed the whole game for me. As I learned to "play" with my images while looking for something that spoke to me, I came to appreciate photography as an art form, a form of expression, a way to express how I felt or what I thought. I also learned that the act of making photographs affected my state of mind because the rest of my world dropped away when I raised my camera to take a picture.

I read a lot of artist statements in my work as a journal editor. After reading a dozen or so—believe me—you've read them all. Very few people have anything original to say. Photographers want to reveal the extraordinary in the ordinary; they want people to see things in a different way; they want people to see and appreciate the wonders of nature. I wasn't sure what to say in my artist statement, but one day I realized I had to simply be honest. I make photographs because it makes me feel good. My motives are entirely selfish. I'm not doing it for someone else; I'm doing it for me. It feels really good to take notice of something in my environs, to lift the camera (these days a Pentax DSLR) and frame what I'm looking at in the viewfinder, and then click the shutter to make the camera do its part. What perhaps matters most is that I can look at the image again and return to it weeks and years later and experience that same good feeling, that same sense that it's perfect, that I saw something that connected with my spirit. I became part of it, and it became part of me. We had a moment, one might say. The way I see it is that over time, a photographer gathers an entire collection of moments.

I "met" Naomi Beth Wakan about ten years ago through the miracle of technology. She discovered the journal I edit and publish, *Still Point Arts Quarterly*. Over the years, I've published several of her essays and poems and have now also published a few of her books, including a collection of new and selected poetry, *Wind on the Heath*, and a very popular trilogy on Japanese poetry forms: *The Way of Haiku, The Way of Tanka*, and *Poetry That Heals.* Naomi has become a friend and an inspiration. She's taught me a great deal about how to live a meaningful and creative life.

So I was delighted when Naomi suggested we work on a book together. Selecting the images to include was not an easy task. I wanted to include my favorite images, but I also wanted the images to feel like a cohesive set. As we went back and forth, putting images in and taking some out, Naomi wrote one day, saying, "Your photographs are all about place." I hadn't ever used that word to describe my work—place—but Naomi had hit the nail on the head. Place is very important to me, be it the town I live in, the house I call home, the roads I travel on, the places I visit.

When you look at my images, you're looking at my life and what I love; you're seeing bits and pieces of places I have been; and you're catching glimpses of the best moments of my life.

anticipation . . .
that someone will sit
on the bench
and someone will dial the telephone
and those someones will meet

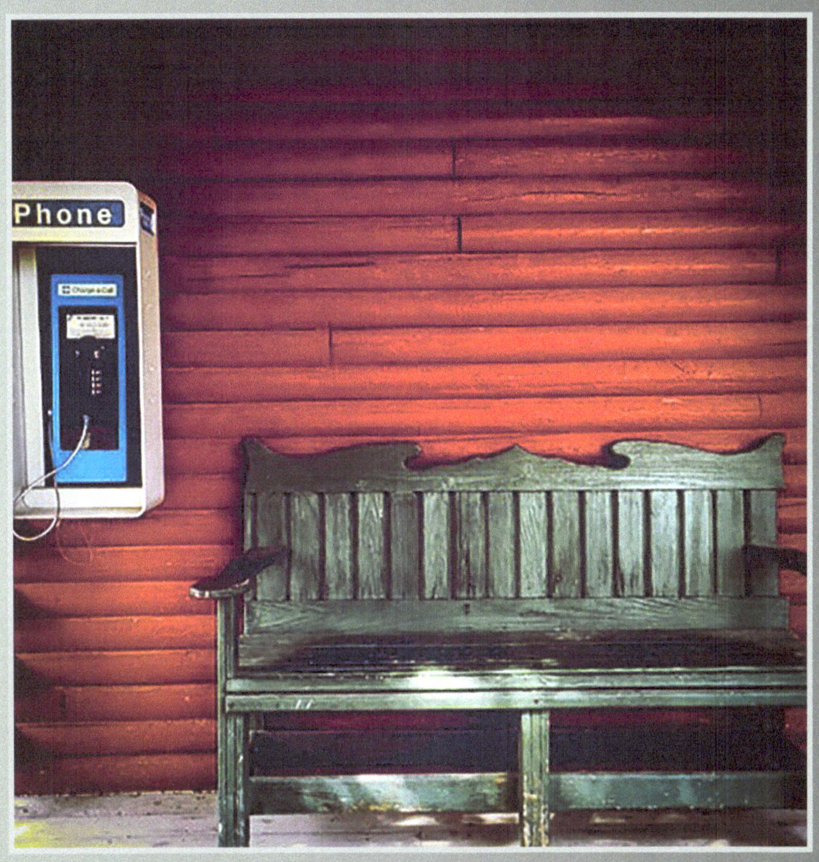
Phone

the first morning light
hits the Autumn leaves'
flashes of color
against the evergreens'
steady greenness

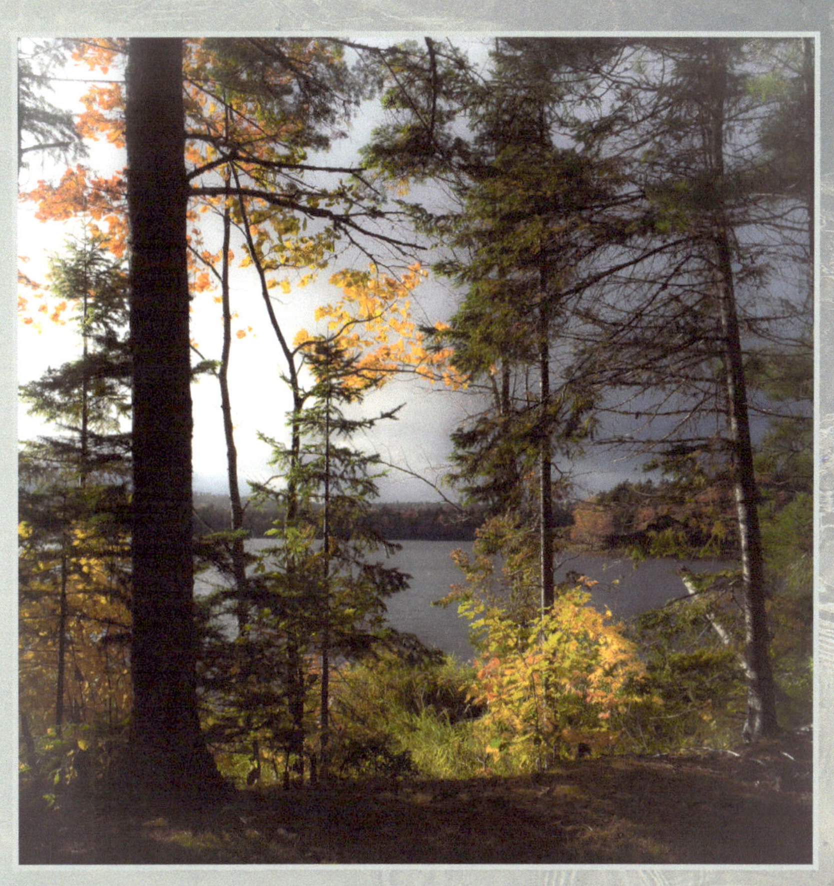

like two lovers
after a pointless spat
the small flowers
look away from each other
and hang their heads

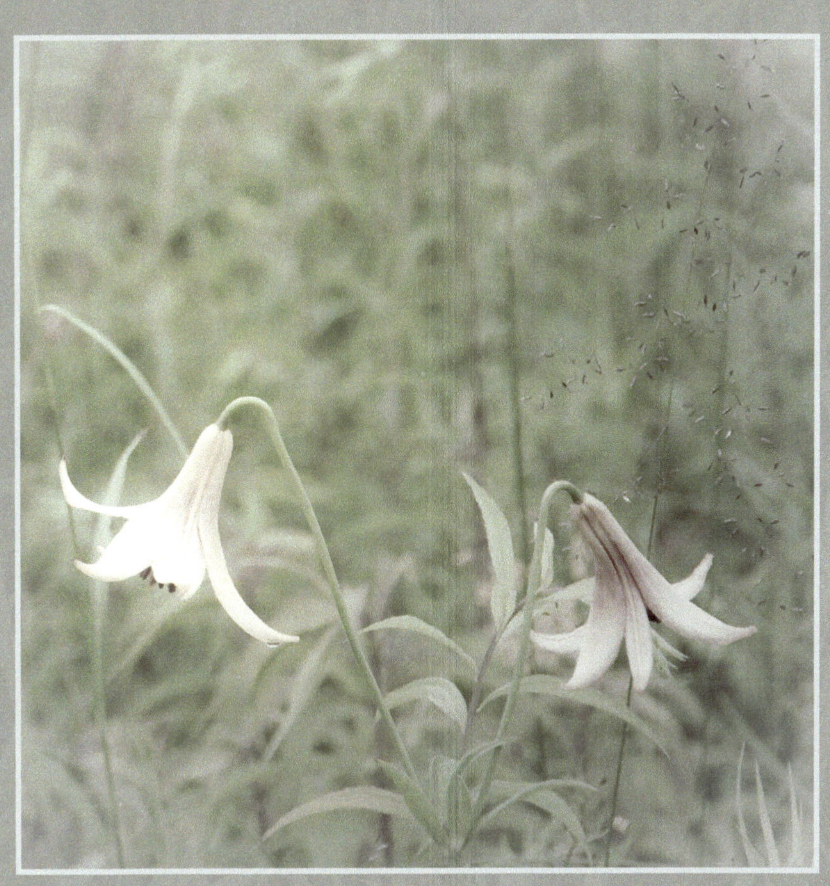

and where
are they now
the alumni . . . ?
some thrive on Wall Street
some are stilled in the ground

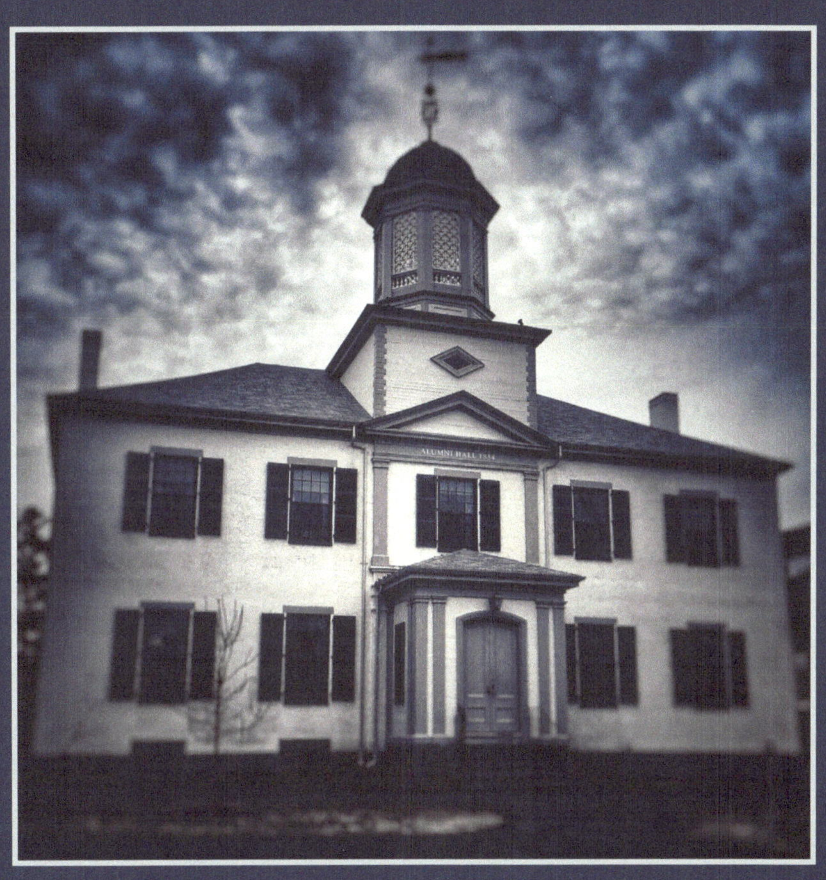
ALUMNI HALL

is there
any sound as fine
as the one
of teeth biting into
a crisp Autumn apple?

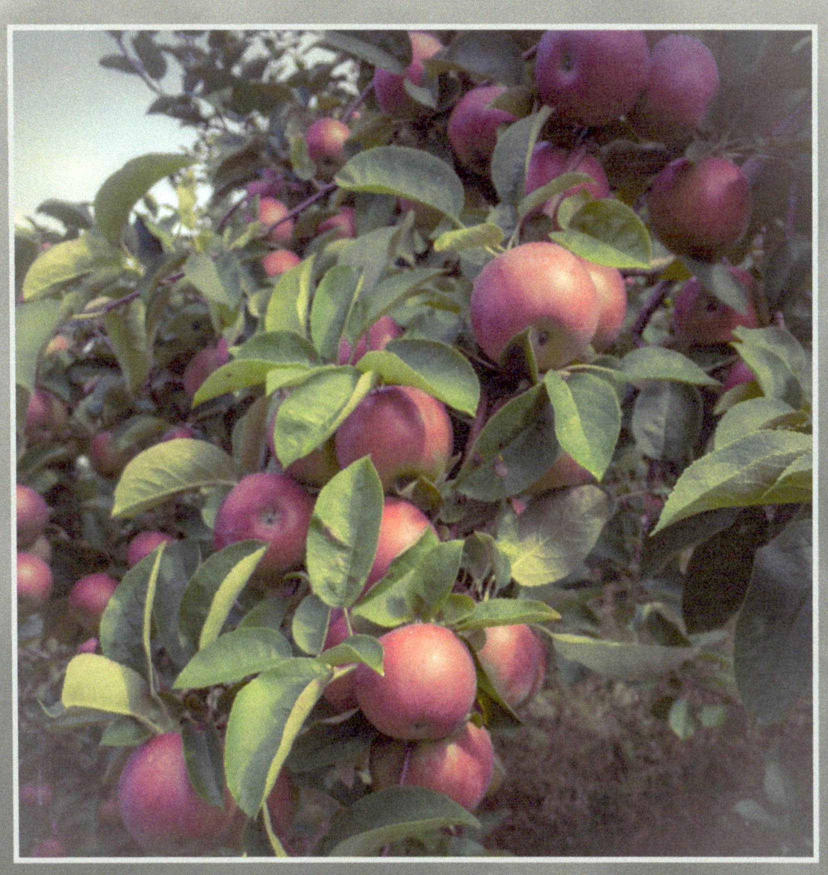

deserted but
there is a story here
in this sealed church . . .
why is it that the number
seems so fresh and inviting?

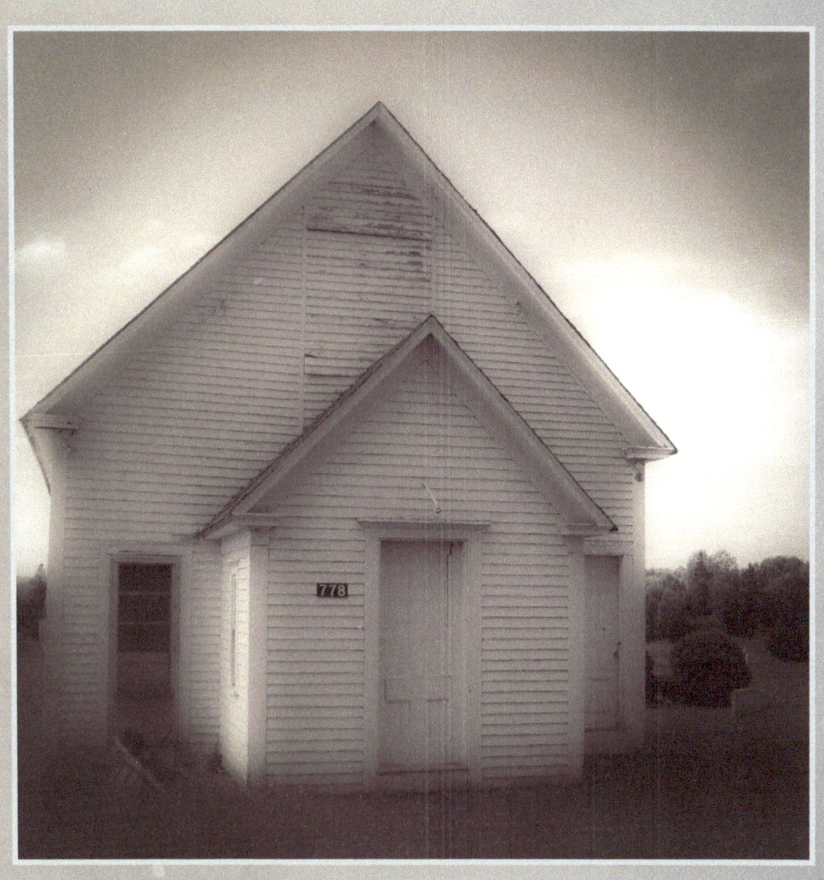
778

early morning
the dew still resting
where it settled
would we could wake refreshed
to look at things in new ways

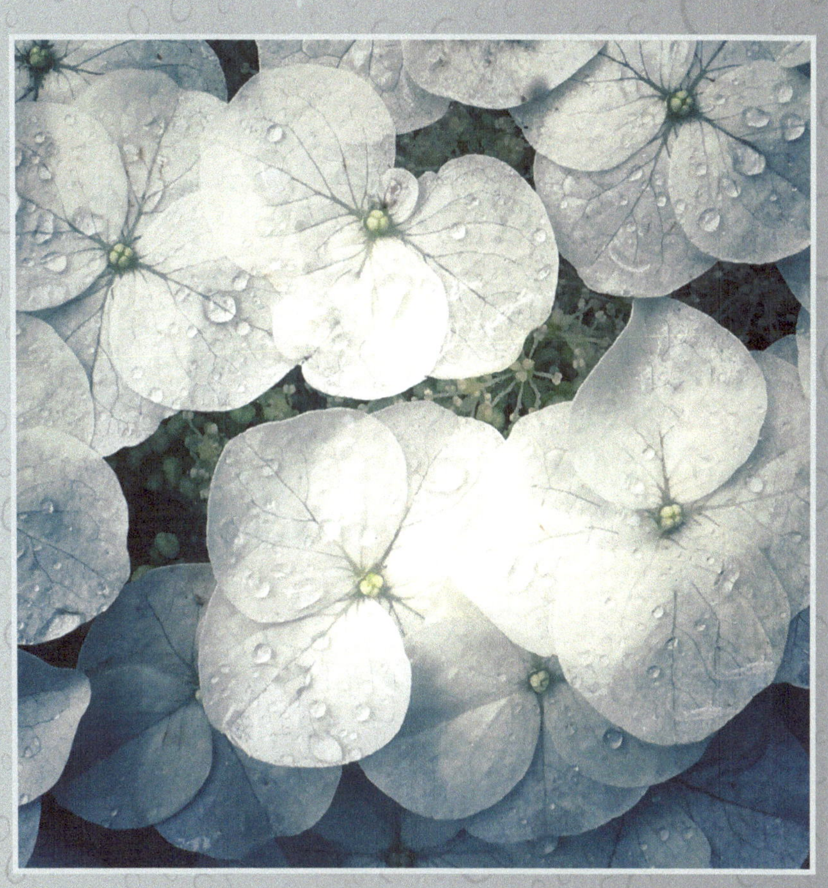

water front park
it's as if the sea-wind
has curved everything . . .
the grasses, the bare branches
even the railings bend leeward

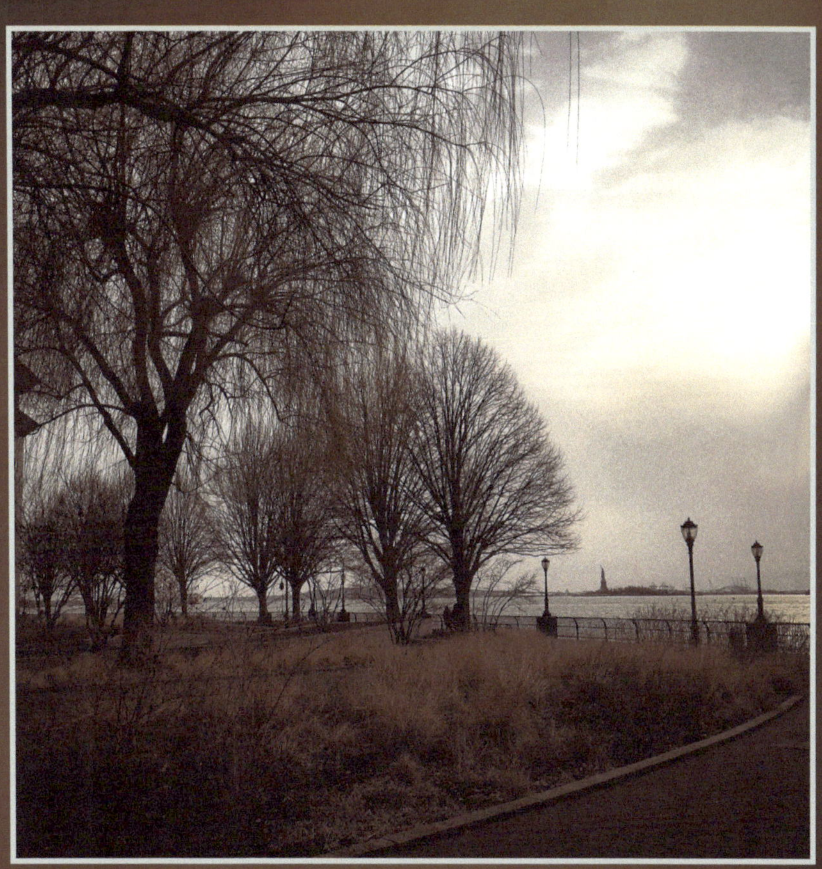

a small white flower
makes a statement
as it struggles upwards
through the mess of grasses
growing every which way

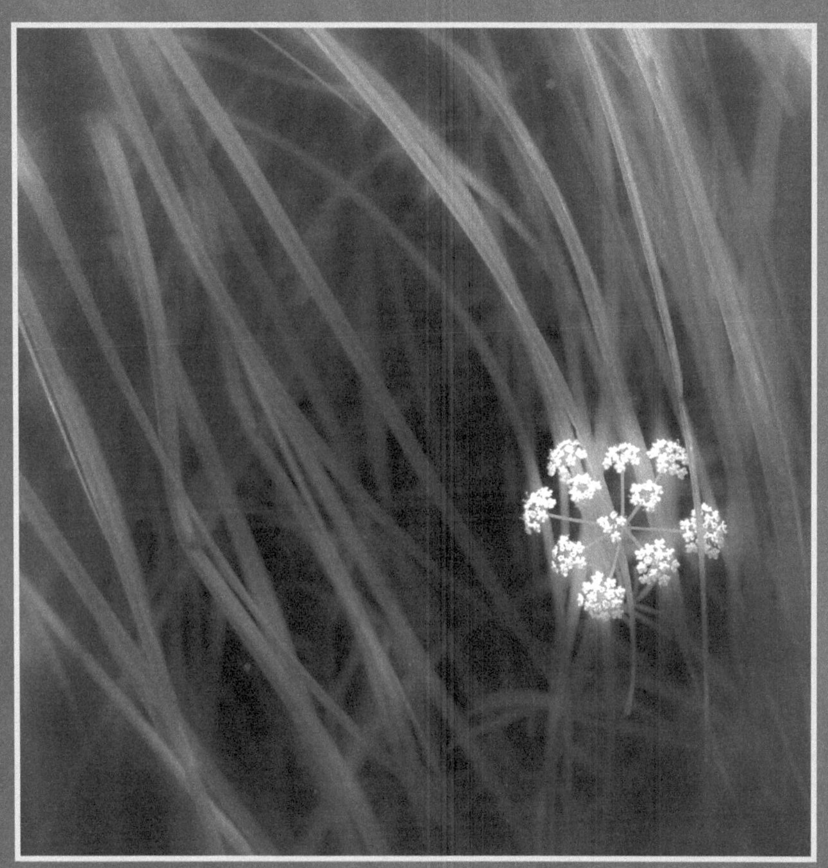

here

children once played

and maybe

there was a barbecue and

cold beers somewhere out back

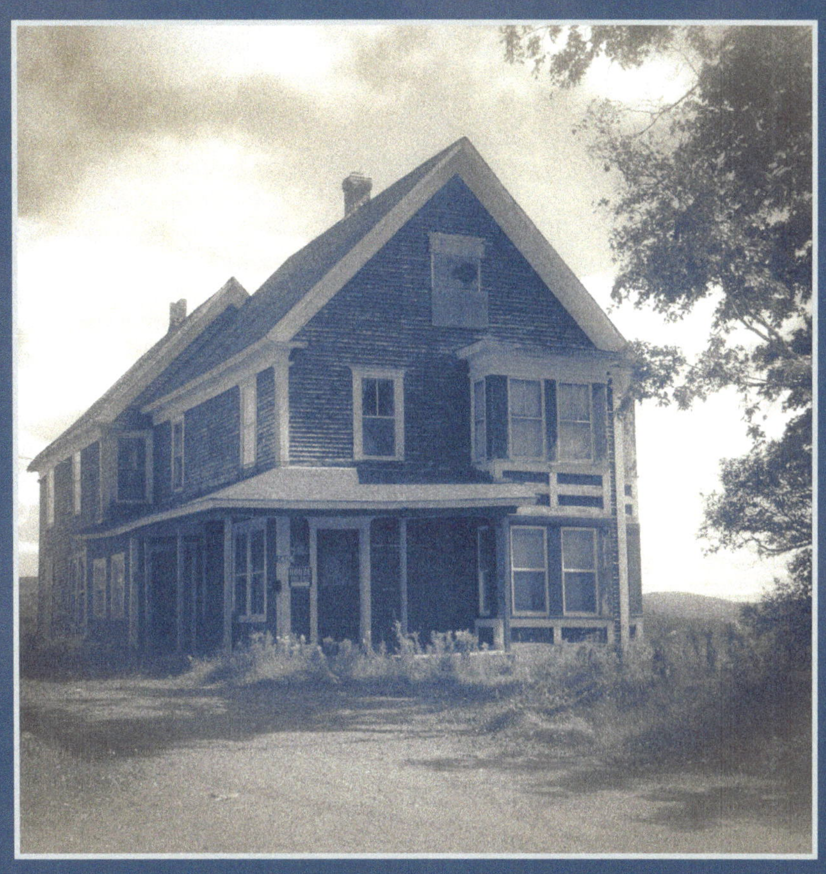

an honest building
and an honest living
and dying . . .
even in desertion
the cabin has integrity

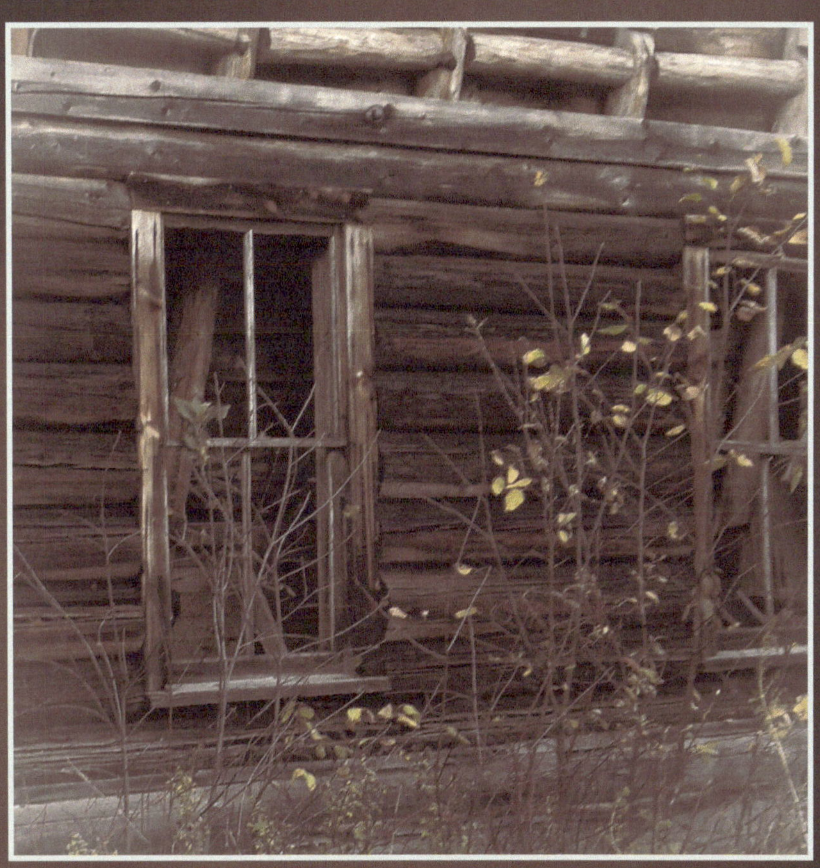

so many movies
start with a shot of
waves rolling in
even a B grade one
signals life's ebb and flow

snow in clumps on the beach
as if some magic wand had stilled
the whitecaps . . .
only spring thaw can release them
to once more dance the waters

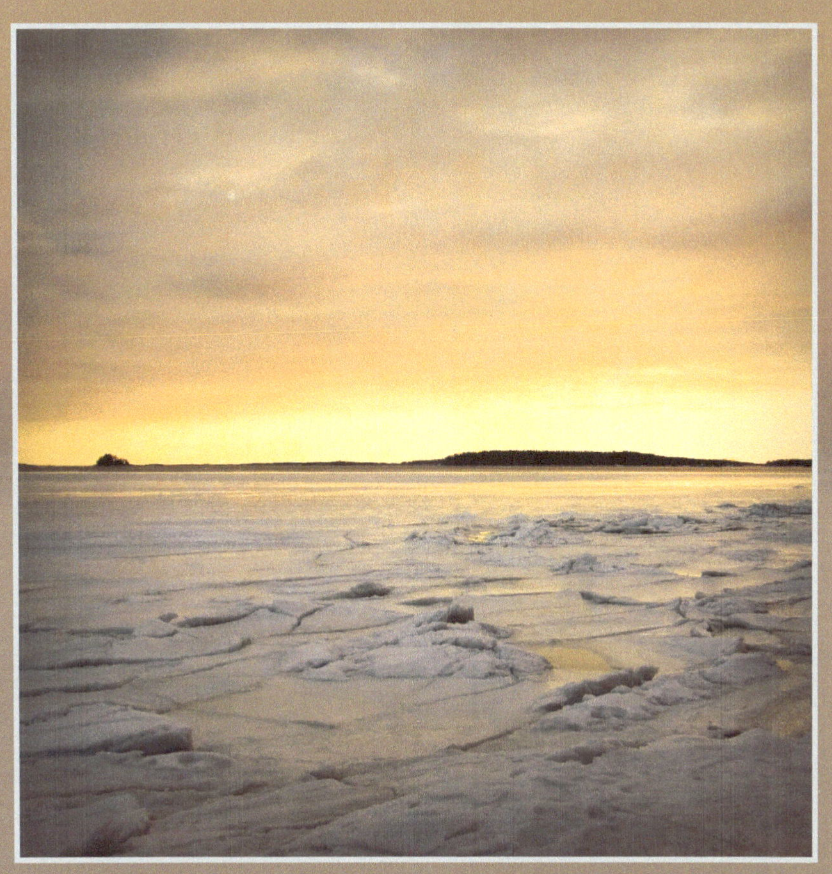

the stillness
is startling
only
the wake of the ducks
marks any movement

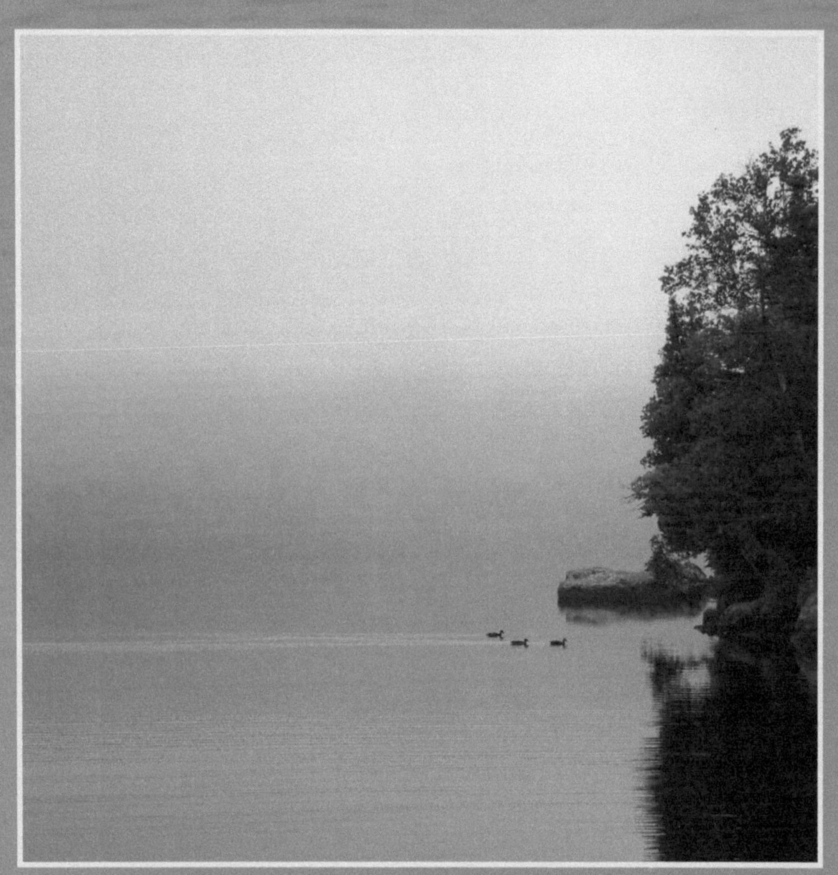

surely
some caring
woodsman
left glasses and cups
so polished and in place

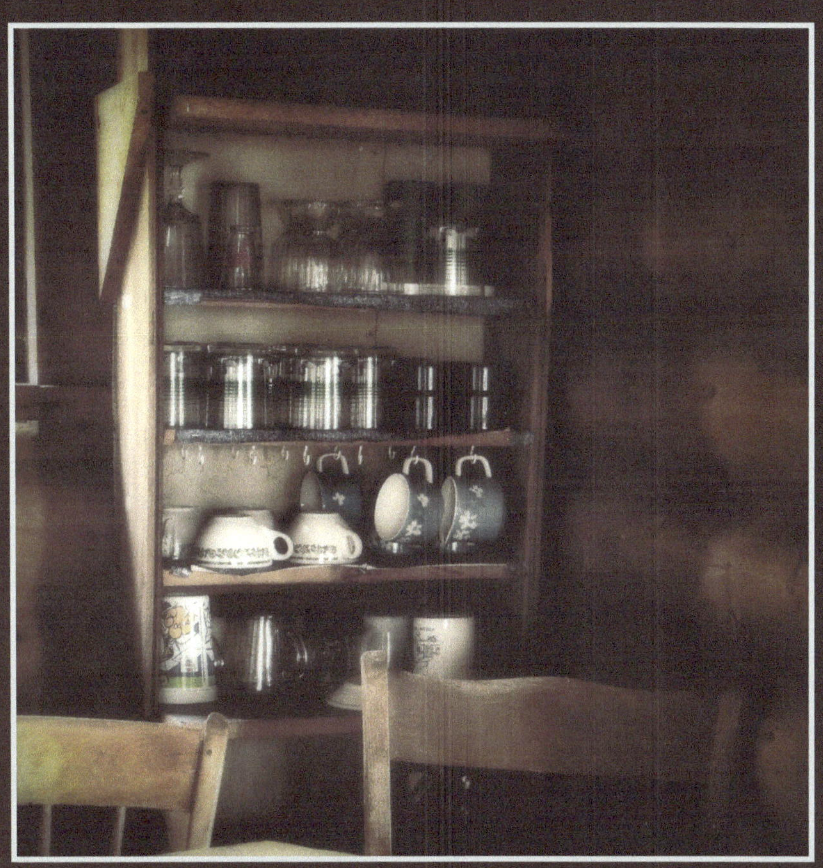

where
have all the tourists
gone?
the emptiness of
a winter sea-side

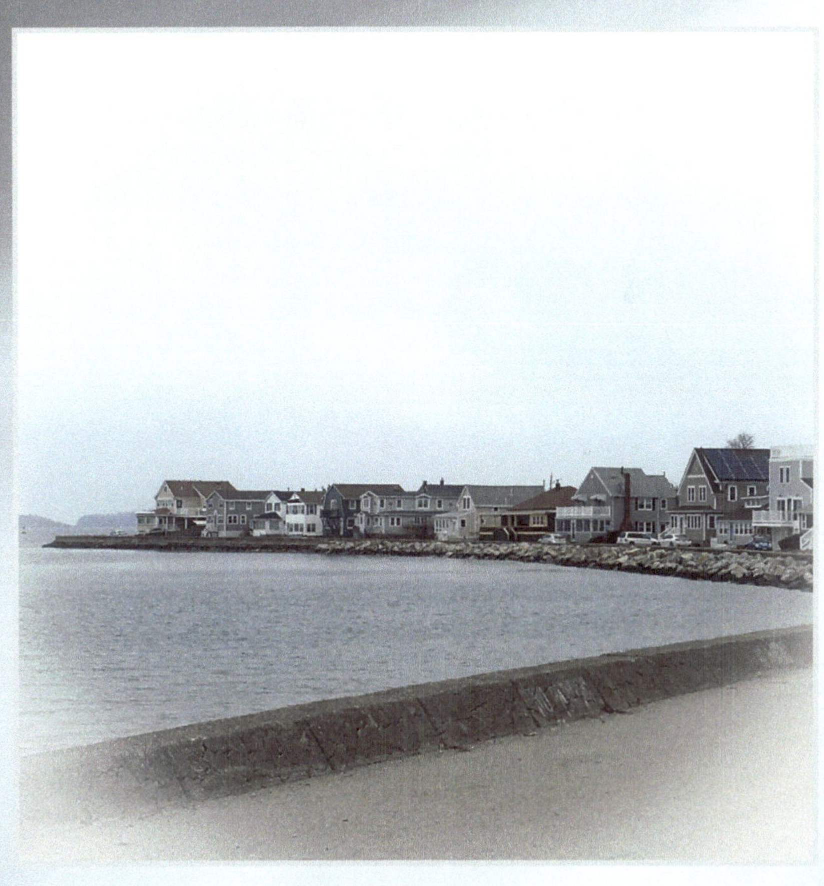

snow piles up against
white clapboard siding
all is white
save a small, defiant bush
its branches gleaming golden

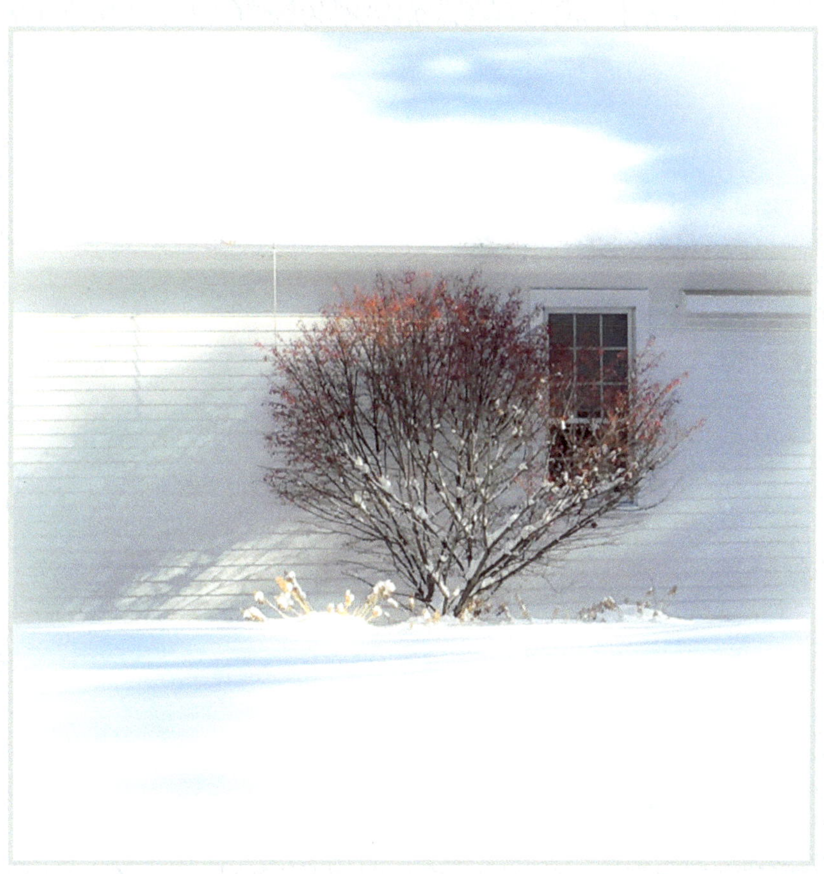

steps
leading someone
from
here to there
are always welcome

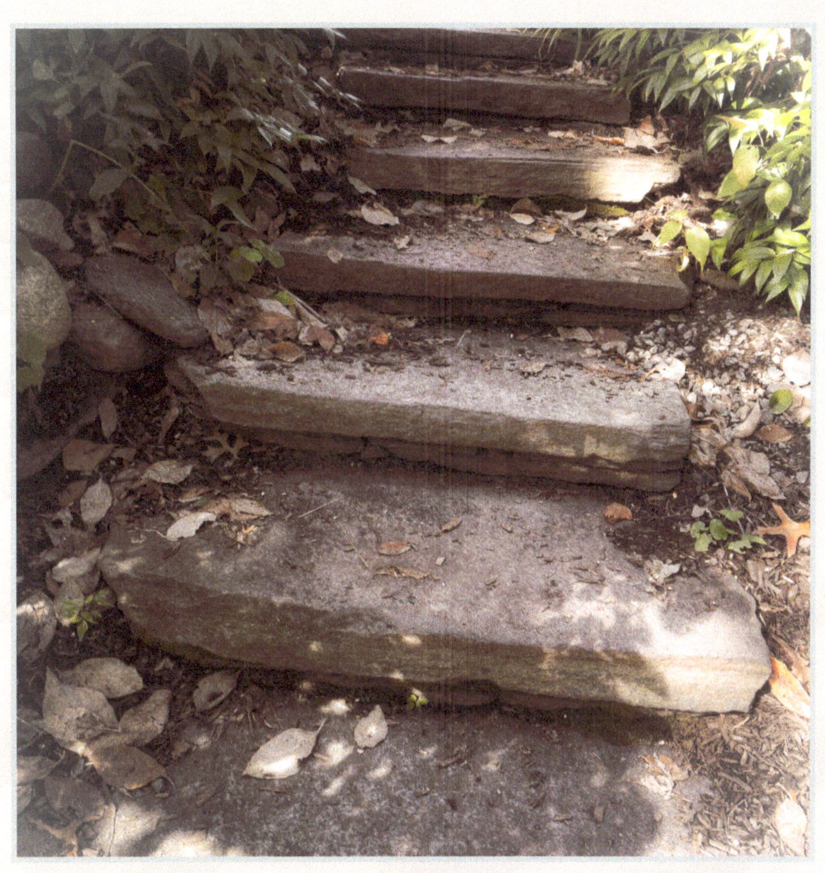

still, so still
not a gust shifting the snow
in the frozen scape
the horizon line, once clear,
has now faded into the sky

a church? a school?
what ever it once was
now it more likely
inspires and educates
a green-starved city-type

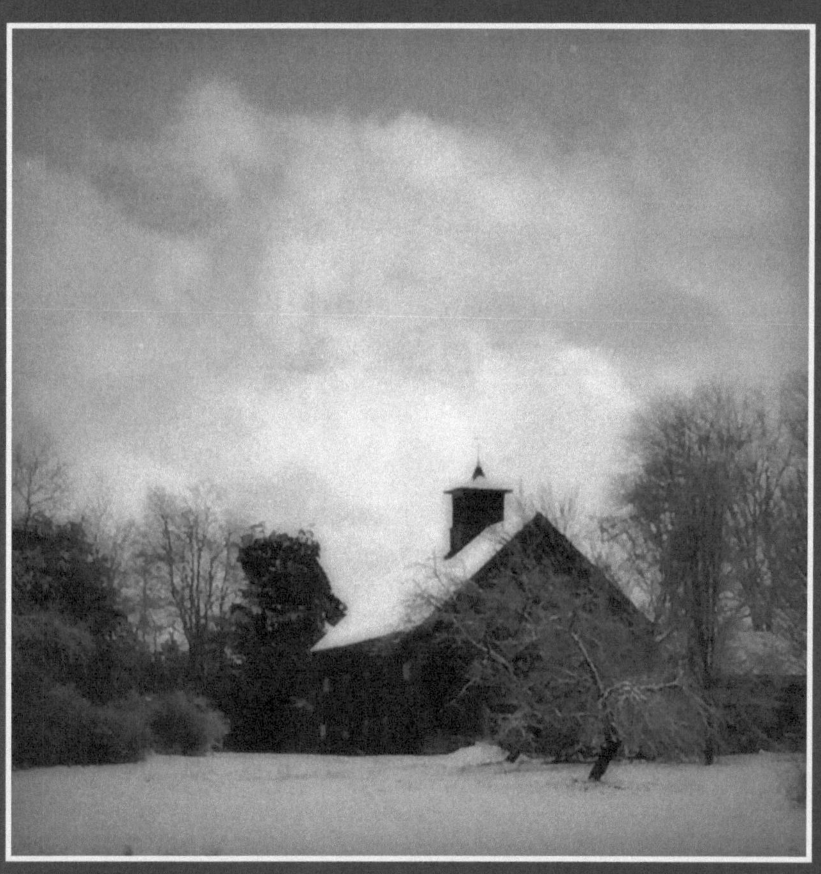

my small-child nose
pressed against the panes
of our bay window
the right, left and center
of the world was mine

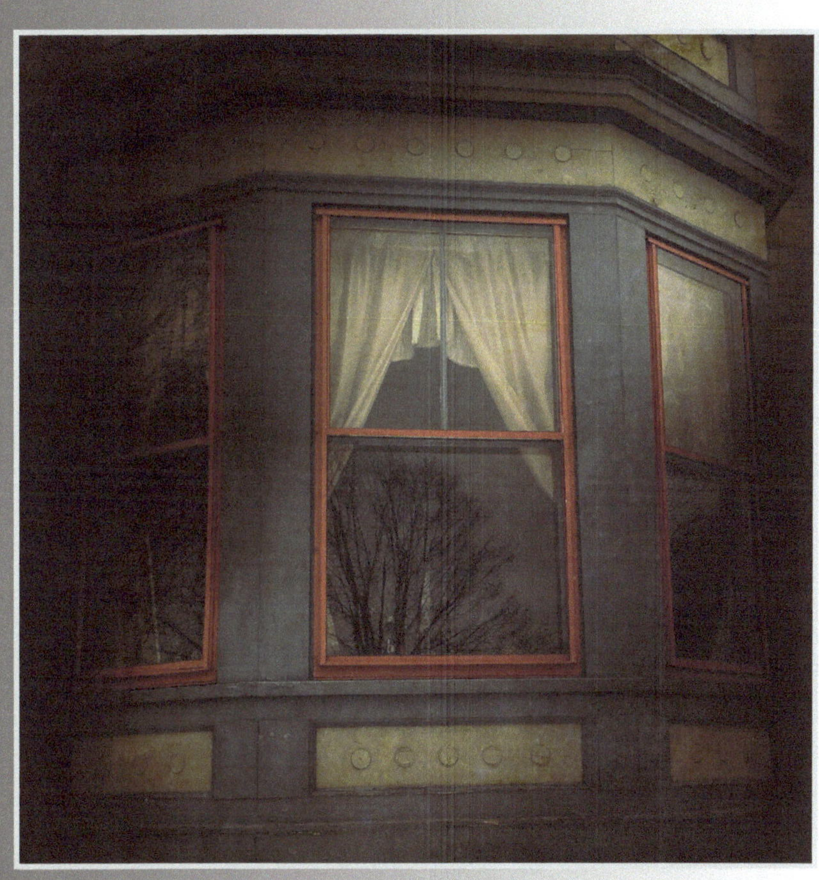

early morning light
and skin touching skin
no desire
just the warmth of contact
and the breeze moving the curtains

the hypnotic
crash of waves
against the rocks
the spume of the breakers
pauses then subsides

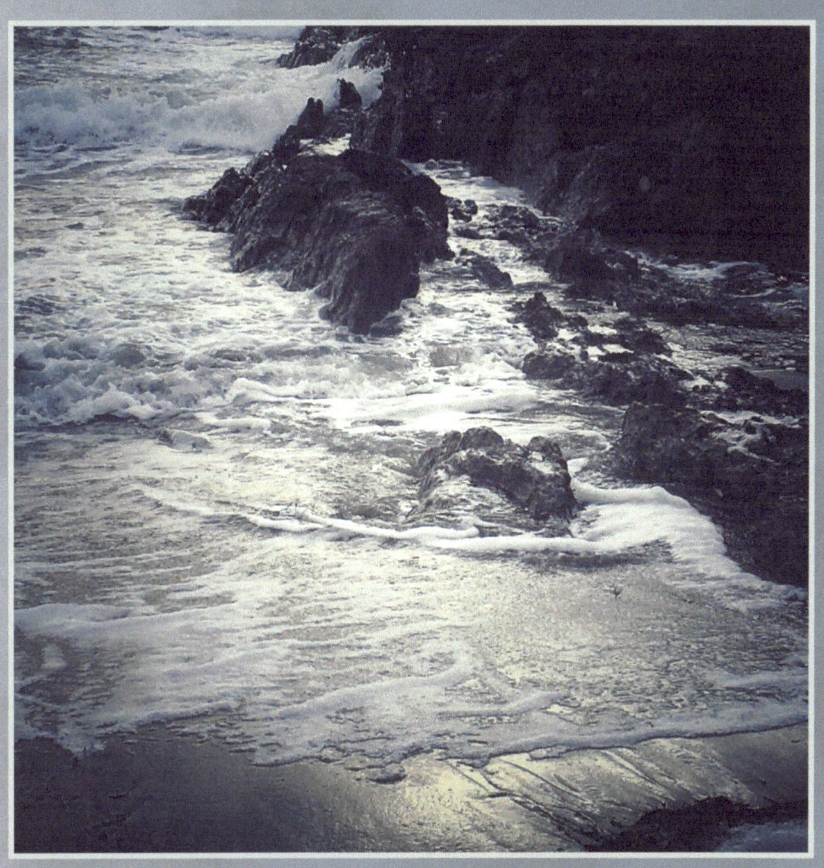

no movement
to be seen yet
underground
the roots call to each other
with friendly warnings

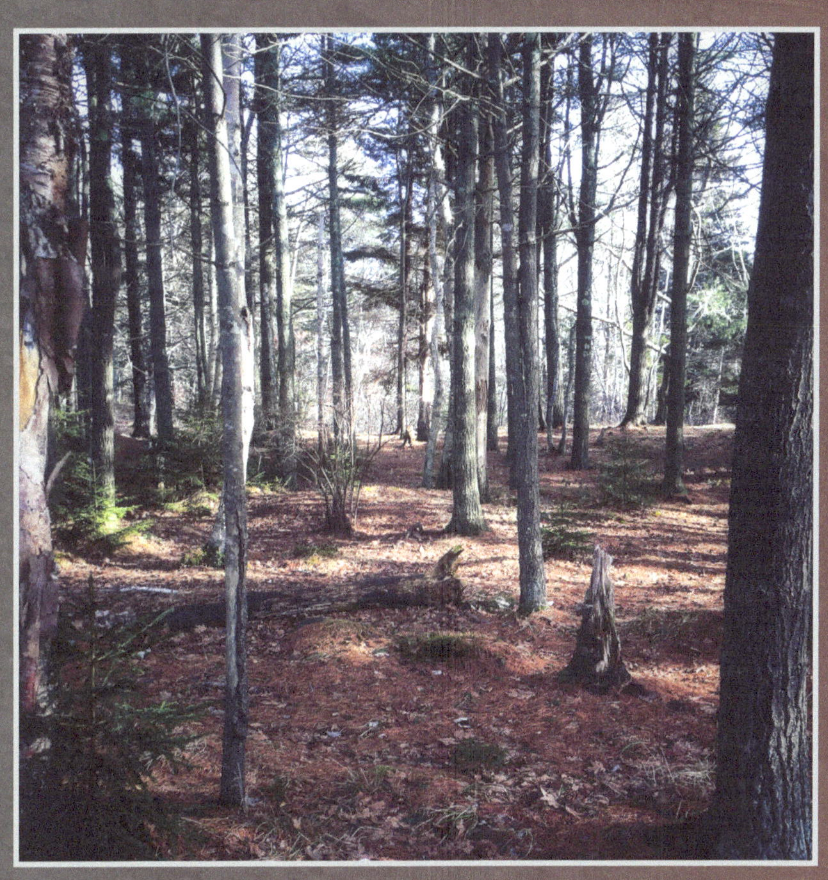

one rising sun
is it ever enough?
the glory
of its reflection
doubled in the lake

what a perfect name
for a donut shop
reputed
as the best in Brunswick
so the coffee-klatch tell me

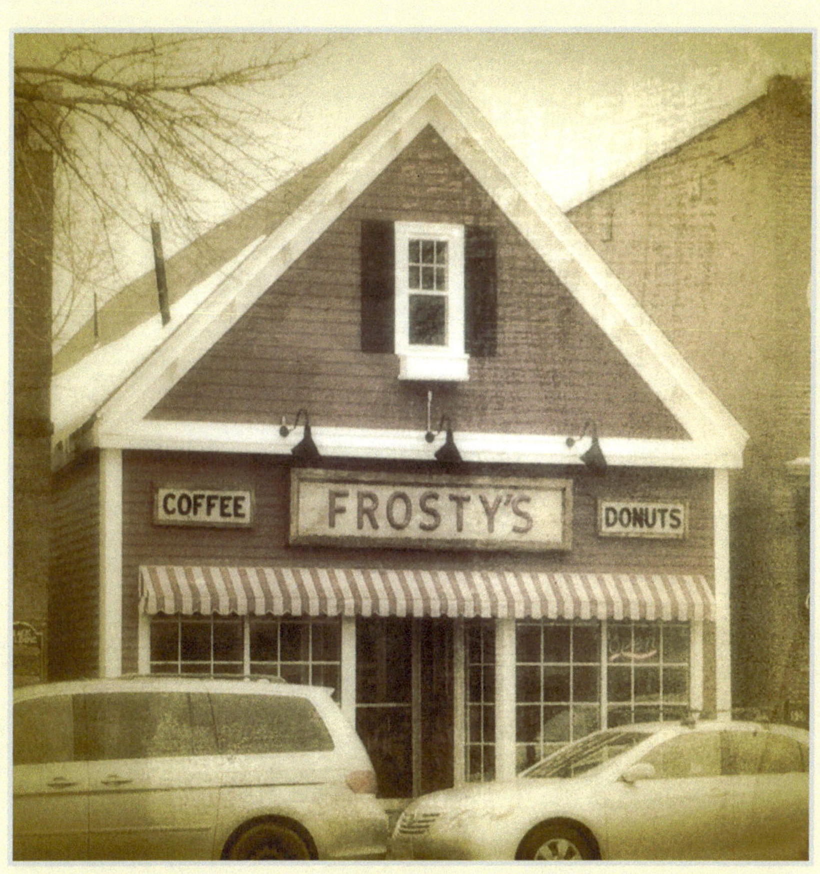
COFFEE
FROSTY'S
DONUTS

after

a forest fire

new growth

do we ever stop hoping for better

times?

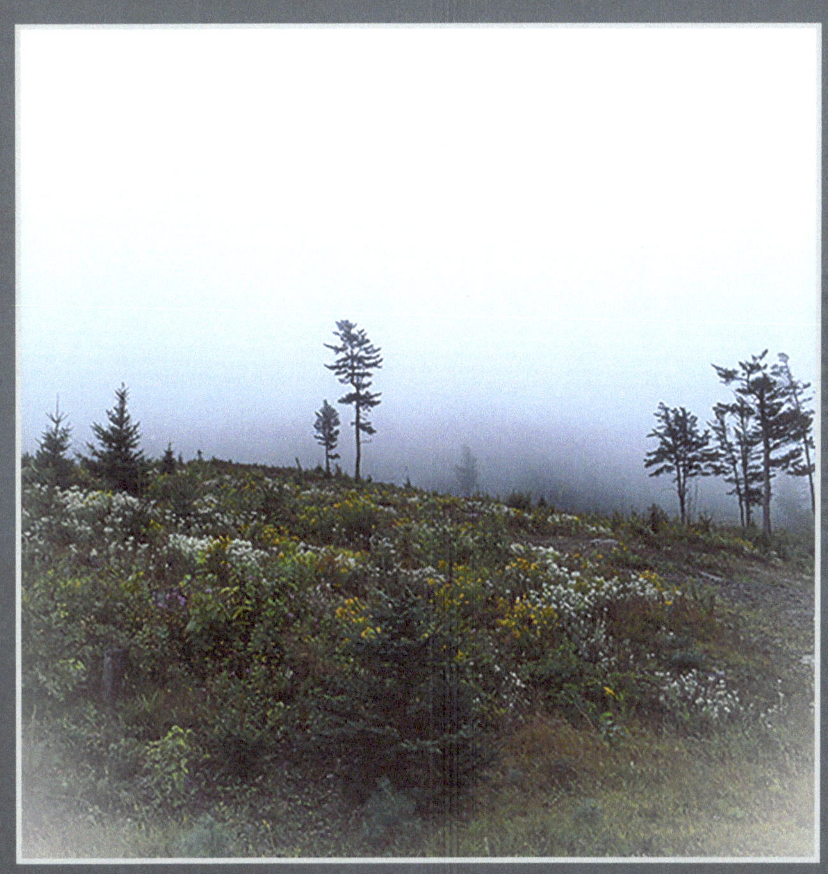

the stunningness
of things that are spare
a simple bowl
wooden spoons in a jar
grass stems against a sunset

at a quick glance
I read FORD, but FRED
it is
and how FRED loves his truck
old and battered both perhaps

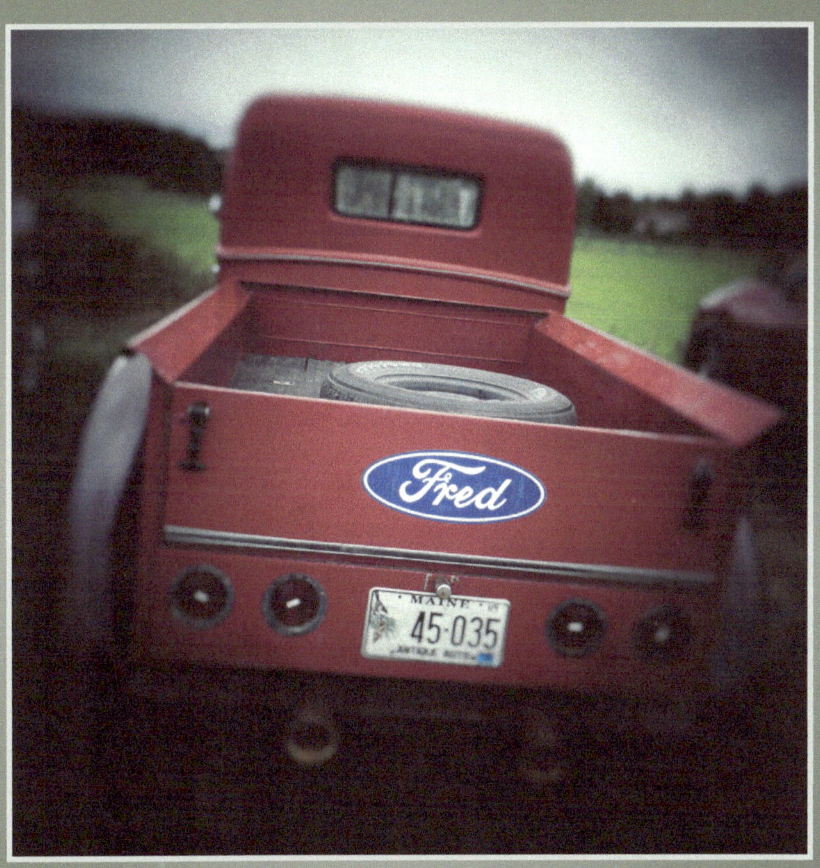
Fred
MAINE
45-035

like a mezzotint
the setting sun
shades
the scene from
dark to light

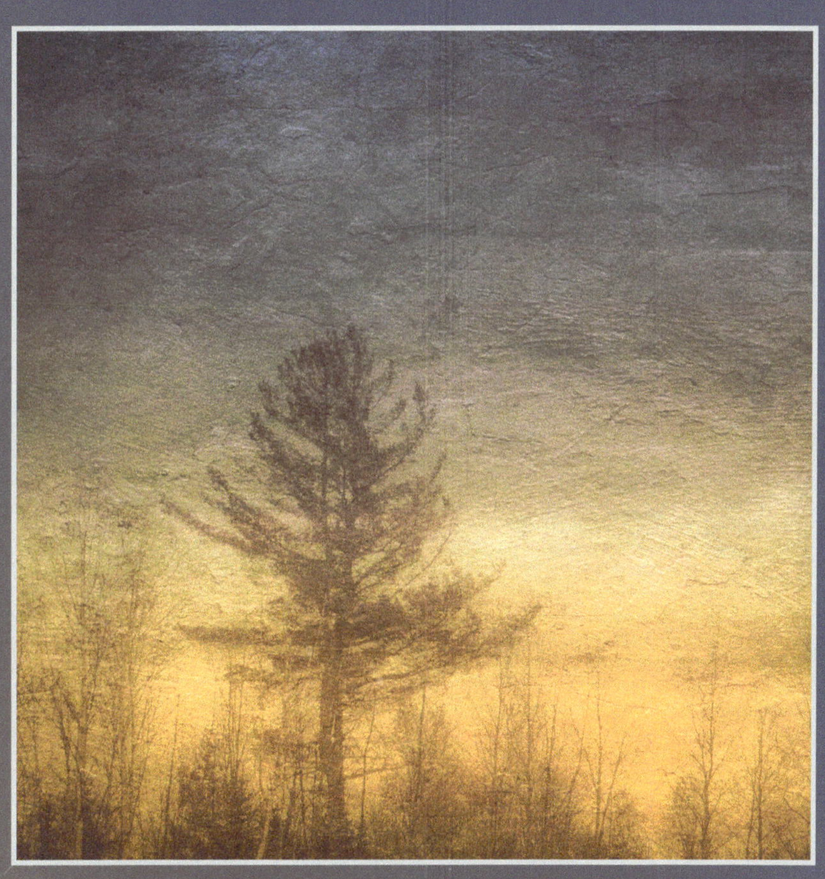

never one
good at naming
mushrooms
I search for words . . . a gasp
then “yellow, yellow”

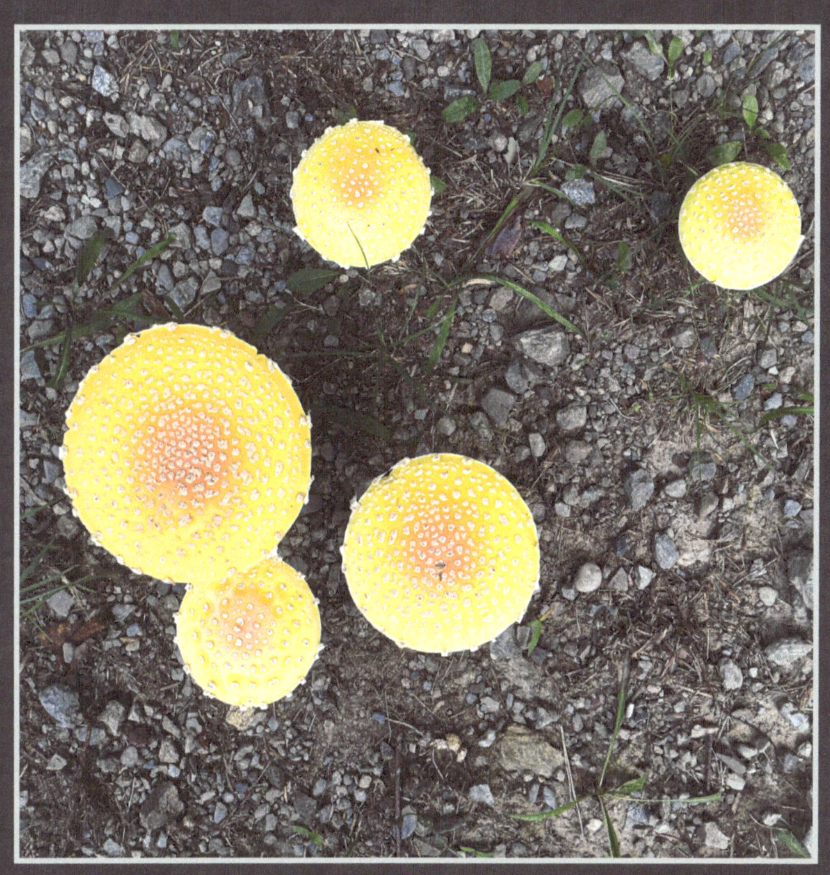

gift of the Incas
is there anything like
a baked potato
with sour cream
and chives for crowning?

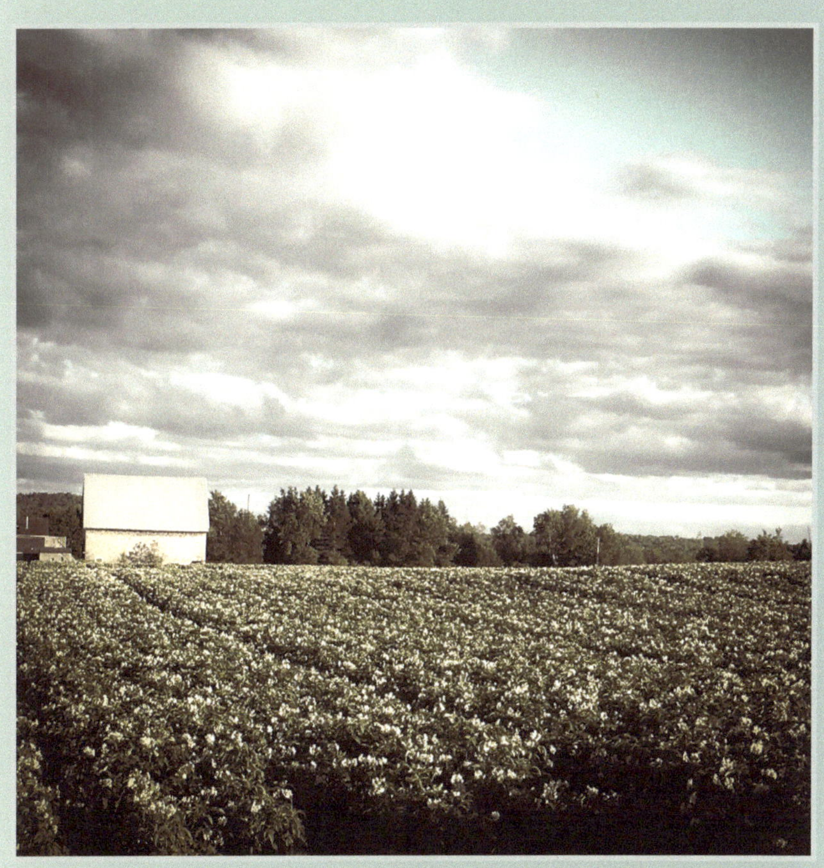

a fresh Fall day
clouds pass above
the russet leaves . . .
does every season
have its perfect day?

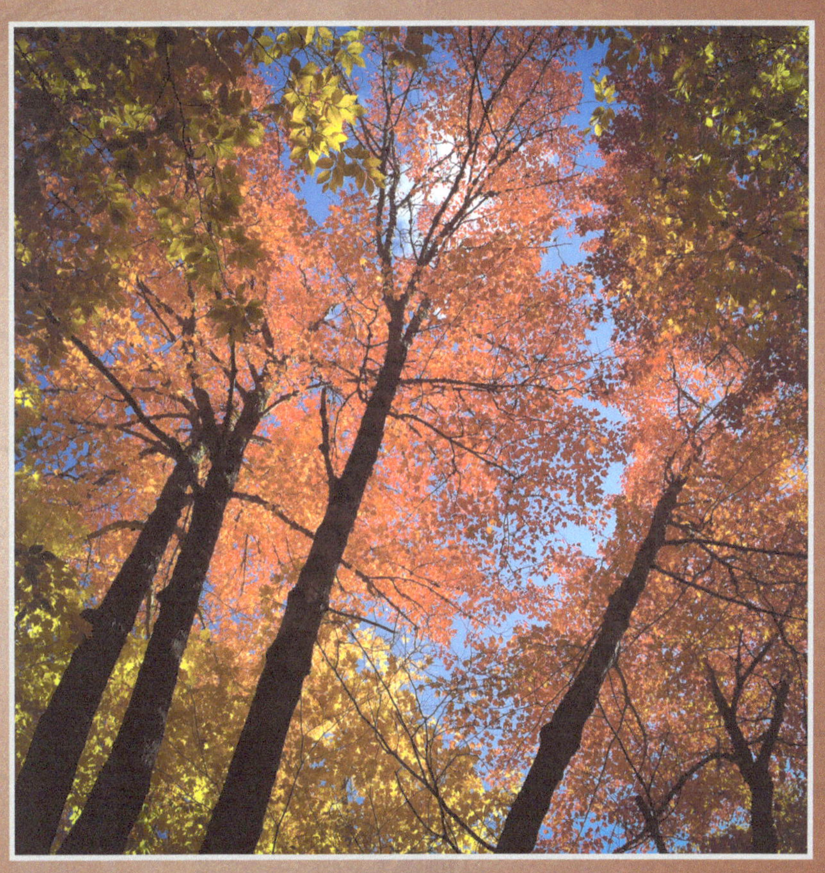

a trim house
a field ready
for planting . . .
why for a moment
do I fear for both?

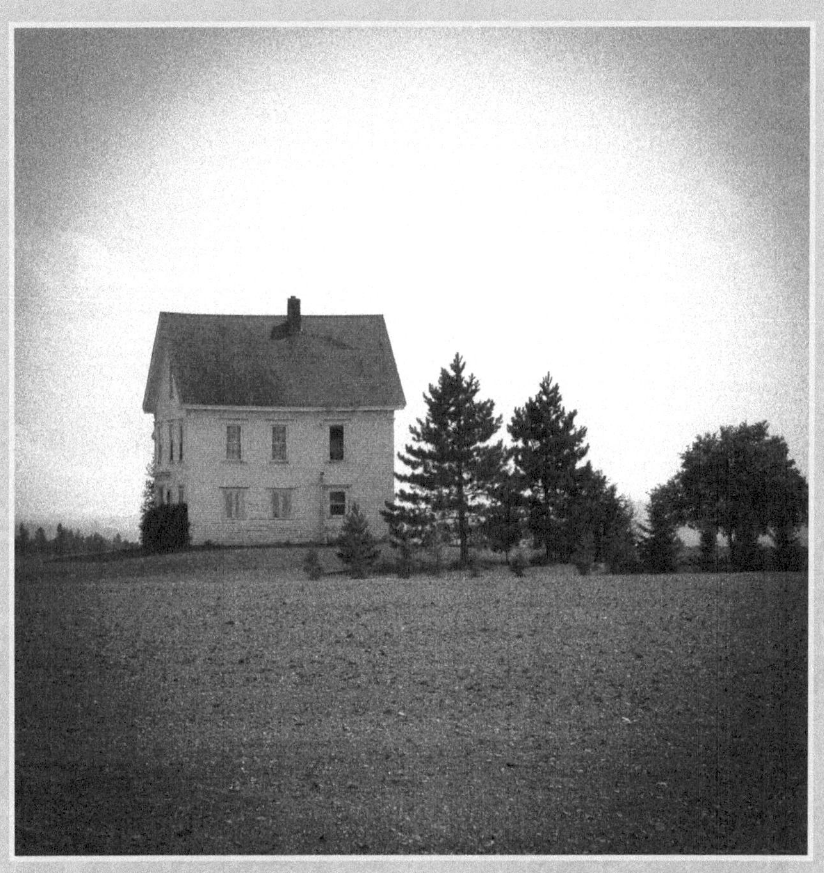

why do tulips
stand military straight
when in the soil
yet in a vase they choose
to tumble this way and that?

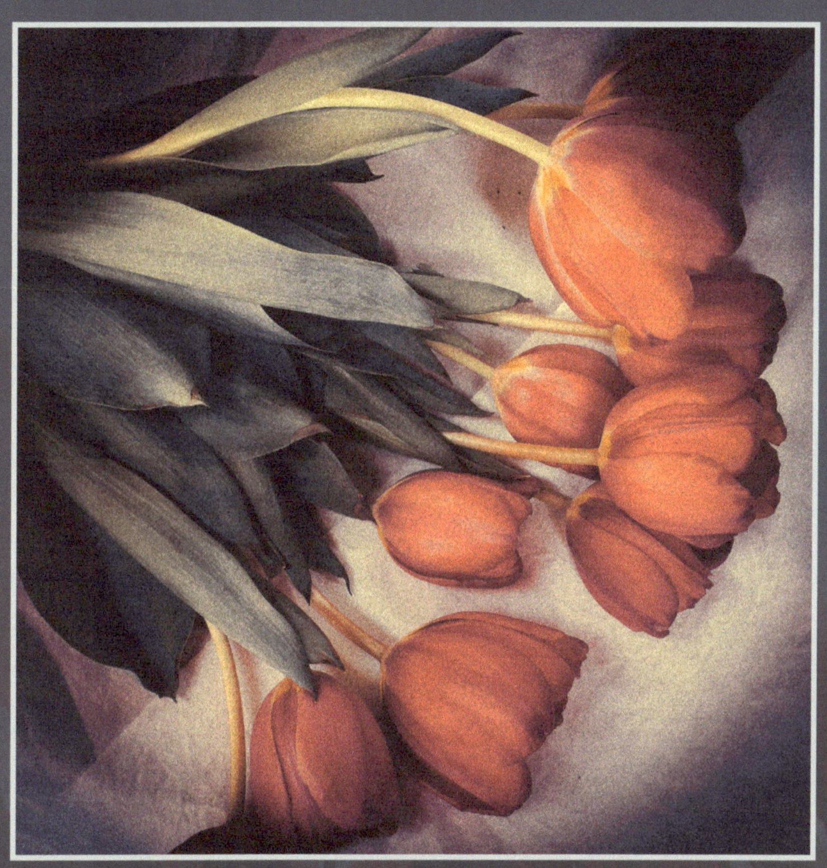

is there anything
as sad as a derelict
building
which once had use
and meaning in folks' lives?

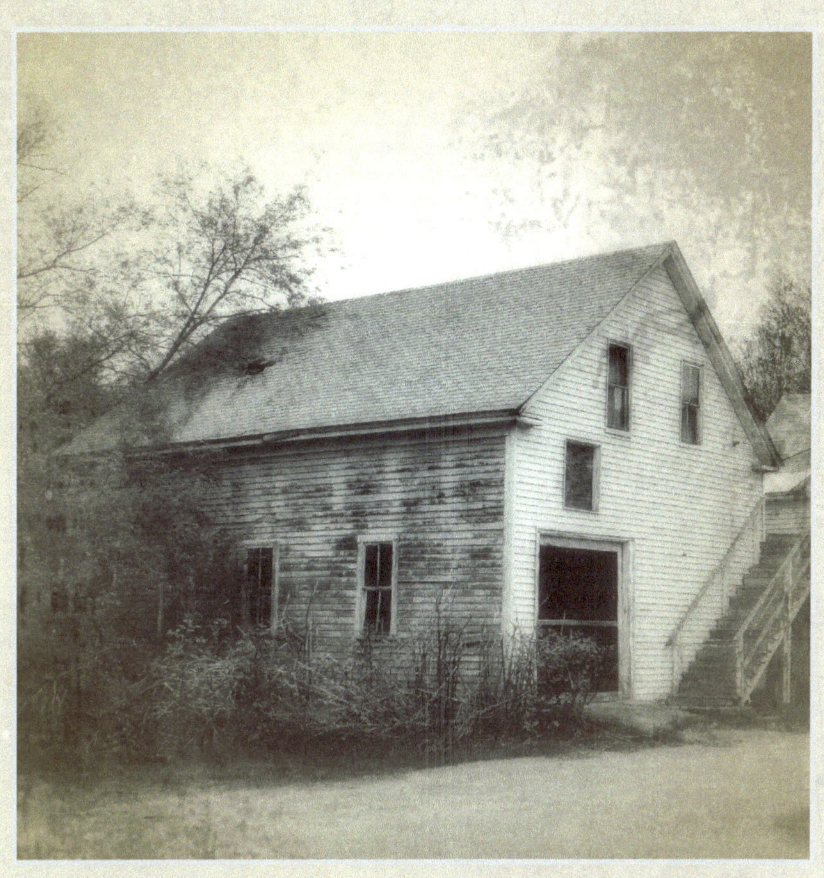

this cherub
guarding over
an Eden-like garden
snatches, for a moment,
an afternoon break

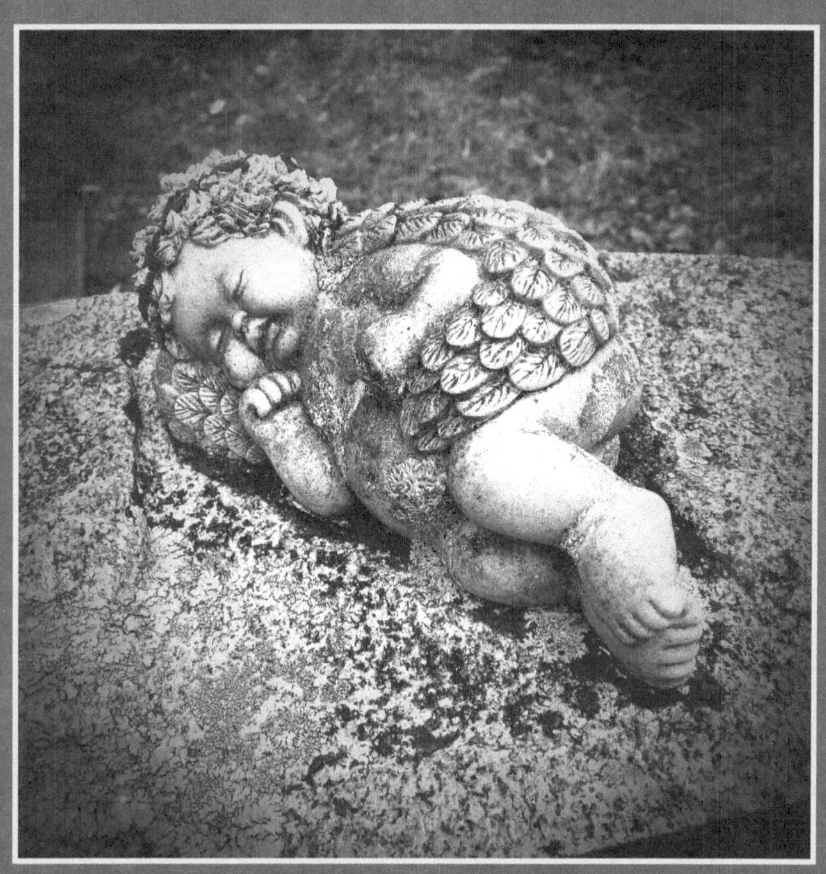

the wonder
of new life
cracking open
two robins start out
on their journey

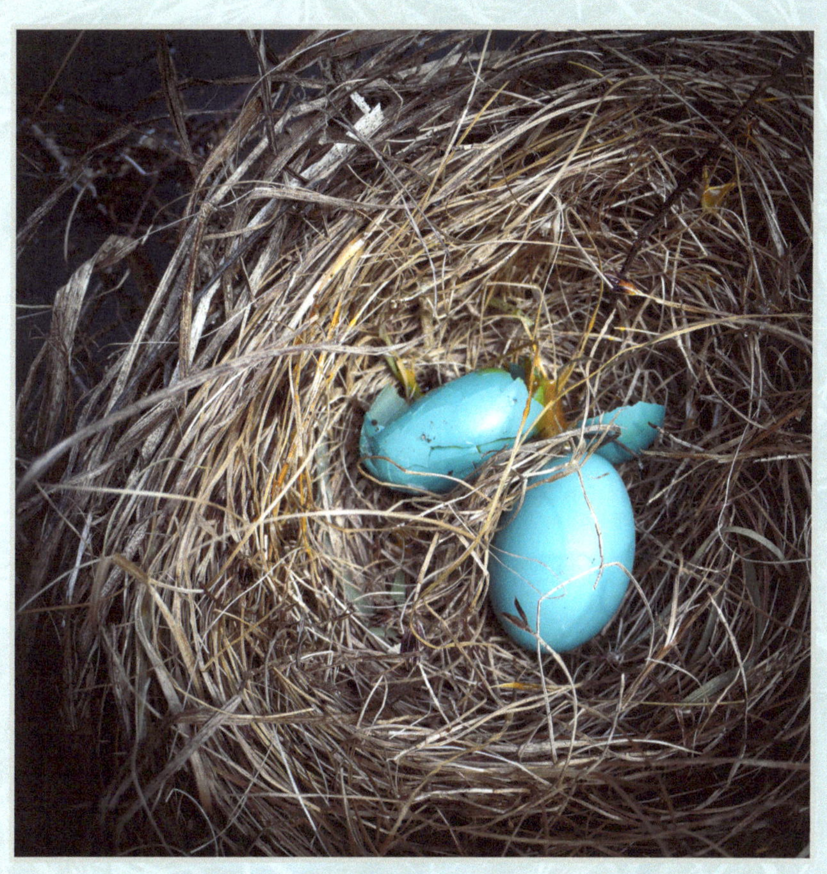

Notes on Photographs

[17] Shin Pond Village, Mount Chase, Maine
[19] Jerry Pond, T5 R7, Maine
[21] Granville, Massachusetts
[23] Alumni Hall, University of New England, Portland, Maine
[25] Rocky Ridge, Bowdoin, Maine
[27] Stacyville, Maine
[29] Location unknown
[31] Battery Park, Manhattan, New York City
[33] Mount Chase, Maine
[35] Island Falls, Maine
[37] Location unknown
[39] Hermit Island, Phippsburg, Maine
[41] Casco Bay from Freeport, Maine
[43] Upper Shin Pond, Mount Chase, Maine
[45] Location unknown
[47] Weymouth, Massachusetts
[49] Nobleboro, Maine
[51] Location unknown
[53] Maquoit Bay, Brunswick, Maine
[55] Highland Road, Brunswick, Maine
[57] Park Row, Brunswick, Maine
[59] NIC Building, Maine Media, Rockport, Maine
[61] Hermit Island, Phippsburg, Maine

[63] Hermit Island, Phippsburg, Maine

[65] Sugarloaf Mountain from the eastern shore of Upper Shin Pond

[67] Frosty's, Maine Street, Brunswick, Maine

[69] Roberts Mountain, Penobscot County, Maine

[71] Upper Shin Pond, Maine

[73] Rocky Ridge, Bowdoin, Maine

[75] North Maine Woods

[77] Mount Chase, Maine

[79] Potato farm, Aroostook County, Maine

[81] Moose Brook Road, Mount Chase, Maine

[83] Route 11, Aroostook County, Maine

[85] A gift of tulips, Brunswick, Maine

[87] Route 123, Brunswick, Maine

[89] Cemetery, Weymouth, Massachusetts

[91] Brunswick, Maine

About the Poet and Photographer

Naomi Beth Wakan is the inaugural Poet Laureate of Nanaimo (2014–16) and the Federation of British Columbia Writer's Inaugural Honorary Ambassador. She has published over fifty books. Her most recent book, a collection of new and selected poetry, is *Wind on the Heath*, 2020 (Shanti Arts). Her trilogy, *The Way of Tanka, The Way of Haiku,* and *Poetry That Heals* was published by Shanti Arts in 2019. Wakan is a member of The League of Canadian Poets, Haiku Canada, and Tanka Canada. She lives on Gabriola Island, British Columbia, Canada, with her husband, the sculptor Elias Wakan.
www.naomiwakan.com

Christine Brooks Cote founded Shanti Arts in 2011 to revel in nature, art, and spirit. Cote draws from a diverse background and wide range of experiences to curate and publish the work of artists and writers from all over the world. Cote edits and publishes the quarterly art and literary journal *Still Point Arts Quarterly*, and designs and produces books of poetry and prose that cover topics from nature and spirituality to music and memoir. She has called Maine her home for the last thirty years.
www.shantiarts.com | www.christinecotephoto.com

www.ingramcontent.com/pod-product-compliance
Lightning Source LLC
LaVergne TN
LVHW052307100826
845147LV00006B/694

* 9 7 8 1 9 5 6 0 5 6 0 9 9 *